The Windows In Dreams

A Poetry Collection

Jyotirmaya Singh

BookLeaf
Publishing

India | USA | UK

Made with ❤ on the BookLeaf Publishing Platform
www.bookleafpub.in
www.bookleafpub.com

Dedication

*Dedicated to everyone who finds themselves within one
of these poems.*

Preface

This book is not a journey from darkness to light, it lingers in the twilight, in the quiet moments where reality distorts and meaning wears out at the edges. These poems are confessions, reflections, and contradictions, whispered by a mind that questions everything yet answers nothing. Read them as you will. Interpret them as you must.

Acknowledgements

These pages hold the echoes of thoughts I could never silence, shaped by time, solitude, struggles, fears, and the weight of my own mind. I owe something to the voices, both distant and near, that have spoken in the quiet, to the books that never left me alone, and to the moments of clarity that made these words real.

I would like to thank my family and friends for standing by me and supporting me throughout this journey. I would also like to thank you, the reader. If you find a reflection of yourself in these lines, then these words are yours now, as much as they were ever mine.

1. Garden Of Eden

Somewhere in the midst of this realm
Lies the memory of heaven
And the fall of the men
Unbeknownst to the brethren.

Once a mirror reflecting Nirvana,
Now lost to the wraith of time.
It was the consequence of the first crime
Which shifted the paradigm.

The serpent, immortal,
Still roams among the humankind.
The forbidden fruit that she dined
Made the heavens leave them behind.

Behold the charade that heavens unraveled
For those who were, are and will.
No saviour, no messiah, just left dead,
Lores were farce to hide the nihilist truth.

The rivers once blessed, now tainted with ash,
Echoing hymns of the fallen divine.
The stars that once whispered the will of the Lord
Now flicker, as if to resign.

The throne of gold is empty still,
The covenant drowned in sand.
The faithful kneel, the faithless rise,
Yet none shall understand.

A voice once carved the laws in stone,
Now silence reigns where prophets stood.
The righteous pray, yet hear no call,
Only the rustling of the wood.

So mankind walks, blind yet aware,
Through ruins of a world once whole.
Seeking answers in shattered glass,
While the abyss devours their soul.

2. Moonlight

l often see a distant light
Burning lonely in the night.
Some call it love's eternal glow
But I have only seen her alone.

As I sat in moonlight with a bottle of wine,
I believed I had no heart of mine
But she showed me where it rested.
Often thought I was rock hearted
But she broke my heart anyway.
Then, she took my heart away
And the city calls me heartless.

Love,
I believe, lives only in tales,
In fictions spun by clever hands,
Or woven in poems of the broken and frail.

I tried to follow, tried to call,
But silence held me in its chains.

What use is love if it can't last?
What good are words when nothing remains?

They tell me time will make it fade,
That even sorrow turns to dust.
But I have lived with ghosts too long
To place my faith in hope or trust.

The city hums, the night moves on,
And yet I stay here, frozen still.
A man who once believed in hope,
Now just a shadow on the hill.

The distant light still flickers on,
A witness to my silent war.
Perhaps it too is just like me,
Fading, waiting, what for? What for?

Tell me, what was it all for?
Tell me, was it ever more?
You must be lost in days lit bright,
While I sit here, drowning in moonlight...

3. Slit Your Wrist

I remember you were indecisive,
Torn between the voices from inside.
Sometimes, I feel the same,
Yet I take all the blame.

You chased answers to hollow questions,
Fixated on illusions that never mattered.
Obsession blurred into infatuation,
Then spiraled into depression.

You were screaming inside your mind,
I could hear you nonetheless.
You survived through all that pain
But survivor's guilt made you insane.

I could have saved you... you knew that,
And I know I have my own ghosts.
We are the victims of Murphy's law,
Life is not like any dream we ever saw.

A caterpillar praises a butterfly,
Does not mean they're different.
Both are the same for a predator,
Both are the same for the creator.

I have wept through endless nights,
But smiled again when dawn was spun.
I thought you stood in that same place,
But you slipped, and darkness won.

I was there to talk
But you left me just a letter
"If my fate and my dreams disagreed,
I will make my wrist bleed."

4. Sisyphus Of Today

I wrote a letter I will never send,
Flipping through old photographs.
Your memories haunt me even now,
I try to forget, but your image still lasts.

The seasons change, yet stay the same,
Each autumn feels like the one you left me.
I trace your name in dust and ash,
A ghostly echo of what no one can see.

The streets still hum with empty sound,
A city moving without me there.
Footsteps lost in shifting crowds,
Yet I still seek you everywhere.

The stars once whispered songs of us,
Now they burn like distant scars.
I drink the dark, I drink the silence,
Both as hollow as the tears of my guitar.

The echoes call but bear no face,
Just voices carved from wasted times.
Would you have stayed if time had faltered?
I still keep you alive in my rhymes.

I dream of you in empty rooms,
Where shadows stretch but never fade.
The air still carries your perfume,
A haunting scent of love betrayed.

If fate is cruel, then love is worse,
A fleeting spark, a hollow curse.
I keep the ashes in my chest,
A pyre built for what was best.

I'd rather be lost with you
Than find my way without you.
Maybe you'll never understand,
And I don't want you to, too.

I'm not living, just killing time,
A fading ghost of burning memories,
Hurting more with every night.
A broken heart has no remedies.

Everything I'm not
Made me everything I am.

Love is the boulder, heavy and grey,
And I am the Sisyphus of today.

5. Flowers Still Bloom

Her eyes made the sun look dim,
Her smile would freeze the time.
Her touch would make heavens rain,
Her words held me away from being insane.

When I'm with her,
I know I can't be dreaming
For my mind can never imagine
The beauty her visage was keeping.

I remember
The night we danced in pale moonlight,
She was dressed in a red royal,
Her face shone and night felt bright.

In my memories,
She still is a raging fire
But also my one and only desire.
Her beauty is something, I still admire.

Though I'm still alive,
I'm not living as I did with her.
Alcohol keeps me alive now
But she could make me addicted with her eyes,
Now, just for her one sight, my world dies.

Flowers used to bloom, when love we'd claim,
Flowers still bloom but they aren't the same.

6. Melody Of Blood

Amidst the peaks and endless ravines,
Cold as the hearts or hot as their rage,
Lies a cavern beneath the ferns,
Known to the ones who recall its age.

In oceans of crowds, all stand apart,
Yet difference makes them all the same.
How cold is the melody of blood,
When shame and silence know no name?

The souls that wander are not of creation,
Hungry for dusk, yet bound to dawn.
No ringing bell, no warning sign,
You long to return, but you are gone.

Man is the fear of what could be,
Yet no light guides where exits fade.
Between nirvana and the inferno,
You learn from the fate your hands have made.

To grasp the spectacle of the world,
To drown within the shrine of time,
Lamentation breeds in all who wither,
Yet strength remains in those who climb.

And in the shadows where echoes dwell,
Whispers of dreams entwine with despair,
The fragile thread of hope weaves through hell,
A haunting song that fills the stale air.

So raise your gaze to the trembling heights,
Where each step forward is laced with doubt,
For in the dance of shadows and lights,
A fragile heart can still find its route.

7. Glasses Of Blood Coloured Wine

Glasses of blood coloured wine
Accompany me in my dark time.
I keep staring outside the window,
To pass time but time goes slow.

I wonder if it's just all in my mind,
I wonder if my thoughts make me blind.
The night I sit awake, waiting for the sun
Is the night I envy everyone.

Glasses of blood coloured wine,
My ever trustworthy friend,
Tell me why everyone I love
Abandon me in the end.

Why does drowning feel like floating?
There has to be a bottle to cure it all.
I killed the man in the mirror
But my shadow still remains tall.

Eyes, the colour of rust,
Vision blurred, unsteady walk.
Past memories unearthed,
Heart static like a rock.

This age, I shouldn't survive.
Buried alive, claustrophobia.
Another glass of blood coloured wine,
Welcome, my beloved melancholia.

Can't afford to feel the pain,
Just want to end it all in a heartbeat.
The perpetual nightmares worsen
Blood splatter all over the concrete.

I'm not living, I'm barely killing time.
Other people's insatiable will to live
Appears like a disease to me.
These people are so hard to forgive.

Sunshine singes my eyes,
The cellar talks with me.
Drowning in a red coloured pool
Seems better than drowning in misery.

Glasses of blood-coloured wine,

Dripping like ink on a torn page.
I pen my sorrows in liquid lines,
Yet silence deepens with my age.

A phantom whispers in my ear,
A voice I swore was left behind.
Memories rot but never fade,
They claw and creep inside my mind.

How many nights have felt the same?
How many dawns have come and gone?
Each one a blade against my skin,
Each one a verse to my swan song.

Glasses of blood-coloured wine,
A final toast to everything that will decay.
The world moves on without a glance,
Yet here I sit, yet here I stay.

8. A Letter To Aphrodite

Aphrodite, queen of love,
The sky and the oceans call out your name.
The poets write of you in gold,
But love still fades, it dies the same.

They say your beauty shapes the world,
That hearts will fall at your command.
But tell me, Aphrodite, if that's true,
Why does love slip right through my hand?

You bring desire, joy, and light,
But love has been such a cruel disguise.
Even though you shine in endless grace,
I only see her when I close my eyes.

She studies with me, she knows my name,
Yet doesn't know the way I feel.
She isn't you, she has no throne,
But still, her presence feels unreal.

Her hair is dark, her smile is soft,
Her voice is quiet, but it stays.
She doesn't have a halo like you,
But I am lost within her gaze.

No doves take flight when she walks by,
No myths were written in her name.
But when she laughs, the world feels right,
And nothing else will feel the same.

Aphrodite, hear my words,
If love is truly yours to guide,
Then whisper softly in her ear,
And let her heart stay by my side.

Let autumn leaves spell out my words,
Let winter winds repeat my name.
Let her remember who I am,
Let her feel my love the same.

But if she stays beyond my reach,
If fate decides this love should die,
Then tell me, goddess, what is love,
If it is meant to end with a goodbye?

You are the one they pray to most,
The goddess lovers believe to be true.

You might be the symbol of love,
Alas! I love her, not you.

9. Pedestals

Psychedelic surrealism surrounds my sufferings,
Smoke and mirrors seldom hinder anymore.
Infatuation and obsession have evolved into depression,
Dead daydreams dragged my soul to deterioration.

Lost ambitions of the past self still breathe within,
Blaming me for the costly consequences.
History haunts me on the verge of hallucinogenic
horizons,
Distant depravity seems closer with correct lenses.

Plethora of pedestals, all rusting after dark winter,
Tell the same undistinguished tales - cynical.
Thrones outnumber the royals by a mile,
Yet sonder's sensation remains superficial.

Corpses worship the guillotine, sheep worship butcher,
Symbolic sentiments remain the euphemism for fear.
Monotonous masochist melancholy marauds morale,
Abandoning the optimist to perpetually suffer.

'Harbingers of chaos' are returning to their kingdom,
I just witness it all as I am a mere poet.
A world burns in my sight, another burns inside,
The abyss lures me, seduces me, I stay devoted.

Eras of errors cycle like cursed clockwork,
The revolution devours the revolutionaries.
Ashes pile on top of old forgotten scriptures,
Prophets turned prophets to mere obituaries.

Steel crowns weigh heavier than gold,
Yet their glimmer blinds the masses alike.
Echo chambers amplify the cries of the doomed,
While monarchs mistake them for songs of delight.

Dissonance drowns beneath orchestrated lies,
Silver tongues sharpened like ceremonial knives.
Serpents shed their skins yet remain the same,
As the cycle of chaos forever survives.

No one await the enlightened fool,
Nor salvation for the self-aware slave.
Empires are built on borrowed time,
Destined to tumble into unmarked graves.

A cosmic jester watches in amusement,

Draped in stars, whispering cruel jokes.
Perhaps oblivion is the purest escape,
Perhaps the abyss laughs as it softly chokes.

10. Shall I Compare Thee...

Shall I be brave enough
To compare thee to a rose?
The beauty compels to withhold,
But the pain of it only beholder knows.

Shall I compare thee
To the white moon of the night?
So far beyond to feel thine entirety,
But still beholding the beauty in leach sight.

Shall I compare thee
To Aphrodite stepping in this cosmos?
Thou nefarious visage is contagious,
But gospels call thine the harbinger of chaos.

Shall I compare thee
To the comet of Halley?
Mankind views it once in eternity,
Yet my heart longs to see thy daily.

Shall I compare thee
To the flames of Pompeii?
A beauty that danced as the world turned to dust,
Yet I'd rather burn than turn away.

Shall I compare thee
To the siren's cursed embrace?
For though I know the depths may claim me,
Still, I dive without disgrace.

Shall I compare thee
To the war that heroes fear?
A conquest where none may conquer,
Yet still, I charge, year after year.

Shall I compare thee
To the requiem of the stars?
A melody sung for lost souls drifting,
Yet still, I follow, near or far.

Shall I compare thee
To the blade that fate bestows?
For love and ruin walk together,
And I shall fall before thee, God knows.

Shall I compare thee
To the doors of heaven?

Dante & Milton praised thou.
You have been the ruin of many a men,
I know I will be one of them.

My lost attempts to use words
to define your existence
have been mine sin.

11. Something's Wrong

Woodpeckers
On a plastic tree.
Such a sorry sight.

Fireflies born in a dark room,
Maybe their own light
Will scare them.

Vultures circling in the sky,
Waiting for something to die,
But they're dying before others.

Humans in the crowd,
Everyone is alone,
Everyone is lonely.

A fish gasping on dry land,
Told to evolve, told to swim,
Told that drowning is just part of the plan.

A canary sings in a broken cage,
Mistaking its echoes for company,
Mistaking survival for a stage.

Scarecrows guarding empty fields,
No harvest left, no seeds sown,
But they stand, as they were told.

Mirrors reflect what isn't real,
A thousand faces, none of them whole,
All searching for something to feel.

A clock ticking in an abandoned home,
Counting time for no one at all,
Marking moments that will never be known.

Paper boats on a dried-up rivers,
Sailing nowhere, waiting for rain,
Waiting for something that will never be.

A lighthouse stands, its beacon bright,
Guiding the lost toward the shore,
Yet no ships remain to see the light.

Puppets dance on tangled strings,
Pulled by hands they'll never know,
Still pretending they have control.

A wolf howls to a vanished moon,
Singing a song no one hears,
Echoing only to its own doom.

An old book missing half its pages,
Stories told but never ending,
A past erased by time's cruel stages.

There's something inherently wrong,
They call this the law of nature.
If a flower bloomed on a grave,
Would you trust it?

12. Addiction

Addicted to the pain,
There is a certain peace in being hurt.
Knowing it is the only thing that is everlasting,
Something that leaves an impression in the heart.

Addicted to the sorrow,
It feels like the world's natural state,
Drenched in guilt, steeped in shame,
Wearing misery like a predetermined fate.

Addicted to the silence,
The silence of the crowded cityscape
Where words are said, not heard,
No words means anything in this world.

Addicted to nihilism,
It was nothing before and will be nothing again one day.
In this boundless tide of fleeting moments,
Every joy is borrowed, every grief is there to stay

Addicted to the fear,
That maybe this is all I will be.
A shadow wandering empty streets,
A name lost to history.

Addicted to the echoes,
The whispers of a life once known.
Ghosts of laughter, ghosts of love,
Now mere static on a mobile phone.

Addicted to the rain,
Each drop like a song of grief.
Falling heavy, cold, restless,
A chorus that never finds relief.

Addicted to the voices
That speak inside my head.
Blaming me for my impending doom
And for the way I have led.

Addicted to the ghosts,
Of people I let slip away.
Their names still burn in my head,
But I have nothing left to say.

Addicted to the lies,
The ones I tell to stay afloat.

That I am fine, that I am breathing,
While the noose tightens at my throat.

Addicted to the ending,
A quiet place where silence reigns.
No more echoes, no more sorrow,
Just a world without my name.

13. A Conversation With Venus

I saw you hanging in the dusk,
A diamond caught in twilight's glow.
The Romans called you love's symbol,
But tell me, Venus, how did they know?

Were you a promise in their sky,
A beacon for the lost and torn?
Did they whisper prayers in moonlit fields,
Hoping for love to be reborn?

I call to you across the skies,
Your silver light burns so bright.
If love is written in the stars,
Then tell me, Venus, am I right?

What is love? A fleeting spark,
A fire doomed to fade to dust?
Or is it carved in stone and sky,
A bond unshaken by time's rust?

And Venus watched quietly,
Giving no answers to me.

How do I know if love is real?
Is it the way her laughter stays,
Lingering like a ghost in my mind
I can not forget for days?

And Venus said nothing,
Just heard what I was asking.

How do I know she feels the same?
Is it the way her gaze holds mine,
Like a secret neither dares to speak,
A pause too brief to redefine?

And Venus remained still,
It didn't answer, probably never will.

If love is all the poets claim,
Then why does longing ache so deep?
Why must the heart, in seeking warmth,
Burn itself before it can finally sleep?

And Venus just shone in the sky,
It did not even try.

Is love a gift or is it fate?
Do we choose or are we chosen?
Is it fragile, is it cruel,
Or just a dream that time has frozen?

And Venus only stared
But it probably didn't care.

And tell me, Venus, if I fall,
Will love be there to catch my breath?
Or will it vanish in the dark,
Another ghost, another death?

And Venus did not answer,
Just watched quietly from afar

I sighed and laughed into the night,
A madman speaking to a stone.
Perhaps I seek in stars and skies
What I should find in flesh and bone.

And Venus quietly smiled at me,
It knew I'll learn it all eventually.

14. I Saw God's Face

I saw God's face
When the sun was high.
The sky was clear,
Yet thunder split the sky.

It was the sound of rebellion,
It echoed through my chest.
A fear so vast, so endless,
As the heavens appeared unrest.

I saw God's face
Hung above the world so bright.
Colossal, distant, wise,
Not a king, but a knight.

His presence held a power great,
Yet I could only stare.
A warmth replaced my hollow heart,
No pain, no weight to bear.

I saw God's face,
A smile carved so wide.
It washed away all evil,
Left only love inside.

He had come for us,
The judgment day had begun.
My feet rose from the ground below,
Ascending toward the sun.

Flying angels called my name,
Their voices soft and sweet.
I saw the others rise with me,
Their hearts at last complete.

Higher still, beyond the clouds,
Only light and peace did remain.
But then the glow began to shift,
And joy gave way to pain.

The sky grew dark, the warmth turned cold,
The air was ripped apart.
We fell like stones from heaven's hands,
Abandoned from the start.

The ground grew cold, the wind grew sharp,
Some shattered where they lay.

The rest were broken, breathing still,
But begged to fade away.

Like the angel cast from grace,
We plummeted through the air.
Was this the fate of all who rose
Or was the heaven's throne now bare?

I saw God's face,
Tears of blood ran down his skin.
The smile once carved in mercy
Now trembled, frail and thin.

Why did he cry?
Were the sins of his creation
Too much for him to handle
Or was it their sorrow and frustration?

I saw God's face
Before it vanished from the sky.
A glimpse of judgment's promise
Perhaps it was a lie.

15. Melting Clocks

The clocks are melting,
Dripping like wax candles.
Seconds dissolve, minutes die, hours decay,
A sign that time itself would not stay.

The sun is drowning in a pool of gold,
The light flickers and everything turns cold.
Shadows rise, distort reality into dark again.
How quickly do we go from smile to pain?

My reflection lags, a second too late,
A face out of sync, a twist in fate.
I watch it fall like a hollow shell,
A version of me I do not know well.

I blink, and years collapse like dust,
Memories rust, moments combust.
What did I lose? What did I miss?
Was there ever more to this?

A watch with no numbers, a pendulum still,
Time bends to no desire, no will.
It drips from the ceiling, pools on the floor,
I wade through time I don't own anymore.

The past and the present blur into one,
Time is beyond anything we can ever learn.
I feel the weight of time undone,
Counting seconds, chasing none.

And when the last clock finally fades,
Will I still know my own name?
Or will I be just another heathen face,
Lost in the folds of time's embrace?

The clocks are melting and so am I,
Drifting slow, too late to die.
A hollow shell, a hollow name,
Dissolving into time's cruel game.

No hands to guide and no path to keep,
The past and the future are the same.
A ghost of moments left unsaid,
I walk through time, most of it already dead.

16. The Fortune Teller

Staring at the ceiling,
Wishing I spend the time wisely.
I keep on chasing time,
But it keeps running away from me.

A crow sat at the window next to me,
"Oh dear aves, what message do you bring here?"
The crow looked around and then spoke
"I have come to warn of your fear"

I was astounded, I leaned near the bird,
"Tell me what fear are you talking about."
The crow looked at my face and said
"Sir, your demise is en route."

My heart grew cold, I got confused
"What do you mean, wise bird?"
The crow waited for a moment
"You have outlived your time in this world."

"Don't speak in riddles, give me answers
For I don't know how much time I have got."
The crow smiled "Sir, you had all the time in the world
But you stared at the ceiling and lay down to rot."

"How dare you speak with me like that?"
"Beware sir, I am just a fortune teller,
I whisper of the heaven and hell.
I know the paths of the grim reaper."

"Perhaps my hour has come, perhaps you are right."
"Do not let grief burden you, you still have some time.
If I were at your place, I would be enjoying it,
Or else your life would cost a penny and a dime"

"Tell me, how can I embrace life if I'm bound to die."
"I told you I'm a fortune teller, not an angel.
I am not the one to show you the path,
You yourself were supposed to make your time special."

"I feel like the clock is ticking faster."
The crow's shadow stretched across the floor.
"You beg for time, yet let it slip,
Now what is it you're pleading for?"

"I wish I would have lived more and enjoyed life"
"But you never moved, just stood in a place,

Now death has come to claim its due,
And you must look it in the face."

"Answer my prayers, dear Lord, I wish to live more."
"No gods will turn the hourglass round.
You chose to waste the life you had,
Now watch it sink beneath the ground."

"I guess it is too late, I was destined to fail."
"You made this assumption seven years ago,
Made misery and melancholy your vices,
Let me tell you one more thing before I go."

"Speak my friend, the fortune teller."
"You might have went the wrong way
But you did come a long way.
You might die but your poems will stay."

"No one cares about those ramblings."
"It is my job to tell you your fortune,
It is yours to make it true while you are here,
Even in the darkest of the hours, the sun is rising
somewhere."

I looked at the drawer with my diaries
Filled with poems I wrote in an era bygone.

I looked back at the window
But the fortune teller was long gone.

43

17. No Saints Among Us

I walk through the city called misery,
suffering and sorrow surrounds me.
Feelings disappeared slowly with time
and I lost everything for a penny and a dime.

I walk through the alleys soaked in rain,
Hearing echoes of whispers, echoes of pain.
Footsteps vanish, shadows remain,
Bound to this cycle, lost in the chain.

Walking through the mirage called hope,
I see corpses hung on a rope.
People abandon the dead weight immediately
after they become free.

We all are self-centred, I'll be the one to admit
we survive this world, somehow we live in it.
People will forget before they forgive
and no one is innocent, no one is naive.

Yes, I admit I have committed sins,
wherever I avoid them, I count it in wins.
But you are not a saint either,
How long will you take to accept your fear?

We build our shrines in pyramids of glass,
Throwing stones, watching them crash.
Truth is a burden too heavy to bear,
So we lie, we cheat, we never play fair.

I see my own sins carved into stone,
Each one a burden I claim as my own.
But tell me and don't play a fool
Are not your hands just as stained and cruel?

The city watches with hollowed eyes,
Waiting for kings, settling for lies.
No saviours walk these shattered streets,
Just sinners praying to dead beliefs.

18. Heaven For Nihilists

Loss of memories,
I forget more than I remember.
Lapse of time,
The clocks tick faster than ever.

Colours do not look as vibrant,
Everything appears monotone.
The sky turns grey,
Even in a crowd, I feel alone.

The sky does not rain as often,
The mornings are not so bright.
After our time has passed,
Will it be worthy of our sight?

Nothing interests me anymore,
No soul sparks an emotion.
I look into the mirror
And yearn to be better.

Every day I lose a part of my soul
As though I stared into the abyss.
There is death around us all
And some perceive it as bliss.

I have given up on myself,
there is a part of reality
that I do not want to see.
Perhaps I was never meant to be.

The world burns everything
It perceives flammable.
We are taught to win or die
Ever since we were in a cradle.

Conversations with hollow liars,
Introspection with no consequence.
Sunshine blocked by smoke
Distorted through broken glass.

Unknown tragedies lie ahead
Even though some have passed.
The darkness keeps on growing,
Keeps telling we aren't meant to last.

After all the books burn down,
Only tragedies will remain.

What a great comedy!
None of the survivors will remain sane.

Heaven for nihilists,
A lucid dream of nothingness.
Drifting without purpose,
Sinking into darkness.

Yesterday,
I faced all my fears.
Today,
They stare back from mirrors.

Cremation of souls still alive,
May humanity burn.
The silence fuels hallucinations,
All ingredients of pain in an urn.

The echoes of voices long forgotten,
Fade into the hum of a machine.
History rewrites itself in ashes,
And the past is left unseen.

A thousand prayers lost in translation,
A million names forgotten in dust.
The gods have abandoned their temples,
And left their statues to rust.

Someday, the clock will stop ticking,
And time will swallow what remain.
A requiem sung by the hollow wind,
For a world that died in vain.

Tomorrow is another day.
Today will not matter then.
World will sink in another tragedy,
Many soldiers will have fallen.

19. Absurdism

In the heart of the city,
A philosopher argued with a clown.
Debating the ways of life and death,
As the crowd came gathering down.

"Nothing matters, no one does,
All will fade and turn to dust.
The world was born from empty void,
And return to that void, it must."

Said the philosopher, cold and grim,
His old eyes like dying flame.
His words, sharp daggers in the air,
Cut through the night with weight and claim.

"If nothing matters, nor do you,
Nor does the breath that fuels your speech.
So why then waste your time
On far future that none shall ever reach?"

The clown let out a loud laugh,
Then spun around with careless glee.
"If all is void, then void is free.
Why fear a world of fantasy?"

A murmur stirred among the crowd,
A man then spoke with furrowed brow:
"Love matters, you are both wrong,
Does love mean nothing to you now?"

"Love?" The philosopher shook his head,
"A fierce spark, a hopeless lie.
Your love will rot, just like your bones,
No matter how much you may try."

The clown then tipped his tattered hat,
His painted grin both false and true.
"If love's a lie, and that lie is sweet!
I'd rather believe this lie, why don't you?"

"But life is cruel," the thinker shouted,
"All ends in grief, all turns to pain.
We build, we break, we rise, we fall,
And all we do is die in vain."

The clown just danced on the street,
His steps as light as a floating leaf.

"If death's the end, then laugh, my friend,
For nothing's left for you to grieve."

A woman stood with melancholic eyes,
Her voice a whisper, soft yet stern.
"But if we dance, and laugh, and play,
Do we not make the fire burn?"

The clown then smiled, a weary gaze,
His painted mask began to fade.
"The game is short, but play it still,
For soon the night will take the day."

"Fools," the philosopher then sighed,
"A painted face, a hollow jest.
Life mocks you all, yet still you cheer,
Delighted as it cuts open your chest."

A child then tugged upon his sleeve,
And spoke in voice so faint, so low,
"If all must die, and fade to black,
Why fear the night? Why dread the glow?"

For once, the wise man stood in pause,
His lips pressed tight, his fist clenched.
No answer came, no words arose,
As if his thoughts had left him drenched.

The clown just grinned and turned away,
His laughter echoed in the square.
"Perhaps, dear sage, you fear the dark
Because you wished there'd be more there?"

The night grew cold, the crowd stood still,
The thinker bowed his weary head.
And in the hush, the clown still danced,
As if the truth was left unsaid.

20. An Apology Long Due

I want to be real to myself now,
No metaphors, no elaborate disguise.
Just the truth I keep buried deep,
Hiding it even from my own eyes.

I have been a nomad at heart,
Stability never felt like home.
I change faces like I change clothes,
Never staying, always alone.

I have mastered the art of hiding,
Perhaps I learnt this along the way.
Or maybe I carved myself hollow,
One secret at a time, day by day.

I had a conversation with myself.
I made a decision after introspection
When I locked myself in my room,
Something that might help avoid depression.

I wrote down words on paper,
A single verse on every page.
Words I never dared to speak,
Caged inside, now freed from rage.

I apologise to you, my mother,
For being the son you never dreamed.
You held onto hope, I let it slip,
And left you with tears unseen.

You prayed for my joy in the dead of night,
But I wasted those prayers, every single one.
I wonder if you ever saw
The stranger you called your son.

I apologise to you, my father,
I gave you nothing to be proud of.
Yet you still believed in me,
When I had long given up.

You built a life from blood and sweat,
Hoping I would carry the weight.
Yet I stood there, empty handed,
A shadow in your fate.

I apologise to you, my brother,
I was never a true guiding light.

I left you to find your own way,
I had my own demons to fight.

You looked up to me in childhood,
But I dimmed before your eyes.
I should have been the hand you held,
Not the one who told you lies.

I apologise to you, my friends,
For the absences, the quiet goodbyes.
I had my demons to battle alone,
While you laughed under open skies.

You waited at doors I never knocked,
Left messages I never read.
And yet I wonder, in my silence,
Did you ever grieve me as dead?

I apologise to you, Time,
I wasted you like you were endless.
Chased illusions, fed my delusions,
Now I stand here just defenceless.

I swore I had forever,
As if youth was a binding spell.
Now I watch the years slip through my hands,
Like sand collapsing directly into hell.

I apologise to you, God,
If you ever listened at all.
You gave me life,
Yet I never found my call.

I whispered prayers in hollow rooms,
Yet never stayed to hear.
If you spoke back, I must have missed it,
Too caught up in my own fear.

I apologise to you, my shadow,
You stood so tall behind me.
Perhaps you deserved more colours,
While my world stayed in monotony.

You reflect the man I might have been,
Had I not chased a false destiny.
Yet even as I try to outrun you,
You still follow faithfully.

I apologise to you, my dreams,
For burying you in unmarked graves.
Now I carry your corpses upon my shoulder,
Like Sisyphus pushing the boulder.

Each path I failed to take,

Each promise I never said,
They whisper in the quiet nights,
Haunting the choices I never made.

... Wait, there is something left,
An apology that is long due.
I apologised to everyone
But I deserve an apology myself too.

I apologise to you, my soul,
I treated you like someone unknown.
Drowned you in sorrow, gave you tears,
And left you to suffer alone.

I put you through torment you never deserved,
Called you evil, wished for your downfall.
A part of me wished you were dead,
Another wished you were never born at all.

Yet even after all, you stayed with me,
Hurt, wounded, broken, but never gone.
So for all the sins I casted upon you,
I beg forgiveness from my own.

I apologise to myself.

21. The Windows In Dreams

The windows in dreams,
They seldom show reality.
They show the hollows of soul,
Something open eyes can't see.

The melting clocks with blurred hands,
The landscapes defying all logic.
The dreams relay a message
Through the lucid world so chaotic.

Shadows of past still stand tall,
The mirrors reflect the darkness
But the windows show the horizon
Where every fate converges.

The faceless girl visits in those dreams,
The raiders of the lost souls do too.
Walking on water, floating in the sky,
Nothing yet everything is true.

Dream world is another realm,
Emotions transcend through it.
The physics breaks there
But the emotions don't conflict.

To find oneself, one must get lost.
One locked inside an unholy prison
Somewhere the light doesn't reach
Can still dream of the garden of Eden

The windows in dreams,
They seldom show reality.
They show you what you need
To understand your soul's duality.

The staircase spirals with no end,
Its steps dissolve beneath the feet.
A path that leads both up and down,
Yet neither fate is ours to meet.

The faceless girl still hums a tune,
A song without a single word.
Its melody is lost to time,
Yet in the silence, it is heard.

The stars collapse into the waves,
A sea of time that swallows light.

Reflections drift across its surface,
But none belong to day or night.

The windows shift, they change their scenes,
Each one a fragmented memory to something lost.
A memory stolen by the immortal void,
A moment gone, no matter the cost.

The clocks are melting in the sky,
Their numbers dripping into dust.
The hours warp, they split in two,
And time itself begins to rust.

The golden city stands ahead,
Its towers built on hollow ground.
It whispers truths that none can bear,
Yet those who wake won't hear the sound.

A hallway lined with endless doors,
Behind them echoes, blurred and thin.
You open one, you find the of yourself,
That you thought was erased from within.

The faceless girl extends her hand,
Yet never asks you to obey.
She guides them through the dream wrought maze,
But never shows you how to stay.

The windows in dreams,
They seldom show reality.
They flicker, vanish, then return,
Forever waiting patiently.